Good Man's Guide

To

Becoming

A

Successful

Cheater

By: Eric James Faulk

Table of Content

Introduction

Let me first start off by saying that I think that infidelity in a relationship is never good. Trust, respect, and communication are the cornerstone in every relationship. I believe that every relationship can become better if both people in that relationship are willing to do whatever it takes to make the relationship work.

Now with that being said, let's be real. Men and women have been cheating on each other since the beginning of time. Women have recently accepted the fact that they too can go outside the relationship to get what they do not receive from their mate. Unlike men though, it has been seen by society that it is not acceptable for women to behave in the manner. But on the other hand, men have been able to cheat and it is seen as somewhat socially acceptable.

Double standards have been evident in the past and still hold true to this day. Is this right? Is this wrong? It takes the individual to decide this for him/herself. Ultimately, what you believe to be right or wrong will come down to your morality, upbringing, and live experiences.

Men will cheat! It's not a question of why, but when? Men are run by the physical aspects of life. We love to see, touch, and fondle any person that we are attracted to. Most times we do these things without thinking about the consequences that may come from doing so.

With this type of thinking comes a need for this book.
Men, if you're going to be unfaithful at least know the
right steps to keep yourself from making a wrong
decision at the wrong time that may jeopardize what you
have worked so hard to accomplish in your life. Look,
listen, and learn.

Chapter 1-Take care of home

Before you go out and make yourself happy, make sure that your home is happy and secure. Many of us men can be so selfish, especially when it comes to our physical needs. We seem to put our physical needs and wants in front of the things that are so much important. What I mean when I say important things, I'm talking about our women, children and families.

The old description of a man was to put everything that he held important to him first and everything else second. When everything was ok and secure, then the man could make himself happy. We need to get back to that kind of thinking so that we can keep our households together and happy, then we can relax, concentrate and enjoy what we are doing when we get our "personal" time.

In this chapter I will give you the requirements that you will need to follow in order to take care of home so that you can take care of yourself later. These requirements that you need are as follow: You need to have a job, pay bills, make love to your woman how she wants it and when she wants it, and last but not least, spend time with your child/children and know their interest.

Have a job. To be a man, no matter what you have heard, you have to be able to provide for your family. In order to get the respect that you deserve from your woman, children, family and the community, you have to have a job. Now when I say a job, I don't mean that you have to be a big time money making man, but it is essential for you to have a job if you're going to be a successful cheater. Any man can sit around the house or apartment when their lady and child/children are gone for the day and try to shoot at every female that walks by the house or hits you up on the internet. No, you have to be more creative than that if you're going to be successful as a cheater.

When you have a job, this gives you access to finance. When you have steady income, you become more attractive to the opposite or same sex, depending on your lifestyle. A job gives you a meaning of purpose every day. When you get up every day and go out and work for what you want and need in life, your woman can say that her man is out doing something positive for her and/or the family. With her feeling this way about you it is less likely that she will be all in your face for what you are not doing.

Your woman will be proud of you and will talk about you in a positive manner. In that aspect, if you have child/children then your child/children will hear that their mother is proud of their father and with that they will be proud that you are their father also. When your child/children look at you in that manner it is easier for you to discipline them. Now, when the woman and children are happy, this will give you the security that all things are taken care of when you're out and about so you can concentrate on what you're doing and who you're doing it with.

Now after you have a job, it is essential that you don't spend any money outside the house before you do the right thing and pay the bills where you stay. Now if you're going to deal with a woman on the side, you're going to have to spend some money on her and do the things that she need done to have to keep her happy. I will discuss that in an upcoming chapter, but right now we are focusing on keeping your household happy and secure. It is essential for you to pay bills in your home. If you don't pay or help pay the bills in your home, then you will never have peace in your home. Having peace in the home is a must so you can go out and do your thing.

Now, if you don't have peace in your home, you're never going to have peace of mind, period! If you don't have peace of mind, you can't concentrate. When you can't concentrate, you lose focus and make mistakes. This is the reason why so many men get caught cheating because they can't think straight with all the confusion going on in their lives. You don't want your woman at the house complaining about why you're not paying bills when you have a job, also you don't need her asking where your money is going and what you are doing with it.

The child/children will begin to wondering why mommy is talking to daddy this way. Then the child/children will get the idea in their head that if mommy don't respect daddy, then why should I? You don't want this.
Go to work, make the money that you can, if it's not that

much it doesn't matter, as long as you're helping a woman out she will be happy, for a while. She will expect you to do more and since you're a man, you will have to, eventually. But if you are capable to take care of the whole household with your paycheck and your woman can concentrate on taking care of the house, this is the best deal for you. No complaints, no worries.

Before you go out and make love, freak, fuck, have sex, whatever you do with some other woman or whoever, you better make damn sure that you give it to your woman how she wants it and when she needs it. You don't want to end up like that Johnnie Taylor song "who's making love to your old lady, while you was out making love". Please don't be that man.

I know that after being with the same person for a long period of time the sex life tends to get a little stale like an old piece of light bread that's been out on the table too long. This is the reason majority of men go out and cheat. We want to experience something new, fresh, and exciting to make us feel like a man.

But as the man in the relationship, it is your duty to keep the romance and heat in the bedroom going. Bring your woman flowers to her job; slap your woman on the ass when she walks by you like you did when you first got together. Make your woman feel so attractive that she won't ever think about getting that attention anywhere else.

When the child/children are outside playing, lock the

doors, go in the kitchen while your woman is cooking, turn her around, get on your knees, pull her pants down or pull her dress or skirt up, put one of her legs over your shoulder and eat the hell out her pussy.

After you're done, unlock the doors, sit back down and start watching TV like nothing happen. Keep your woman guessing and interested. When she figures all your attention is on her, then she won't even suspect that your interest lies somewhere else, thus making it easier for you to go out there and do your "thang".

After you got your woman squared away, it's time to keep the child/children happy and satisfied. This is not as hard as people make it. Children are very simple to please and keep in line.

When a child/children have video games, a nice place to live, food to eat, popular clothing and mommy happy, for the most part they are happy. But to be a successful cheater you have to do more than that. You have to know your child/children and their interest. If your child/children are participating in any activities it is essential that you attend as many of these functions as possible. There should never be a time that you choose your other woman over what your child/children have going on. If she is the right woman to cheat with, she will understand but that will be discussed in a later chapter.

Spend time with your child/children and know their

interest. Play with your child/children and when I say your child/children, I mean your biological child/children and/or the child/children she had before both of you became a couple. Because when you take the woman, you take all that she has. Make sure the children are doing what they are supposed to at school and at home. The last thing you need when your spending time with your other woman is the phone calls about little Johnnie acting up at school or he is not listening to your woman at home. When you're gone away from the house you want to be able to handle your business, enjoy every second of pleasure and get back home without any distractions. You can't do that if your home isn't happy and secure.

Chapter 2-Plan accordingly

Planning is essential in most things that we do in life. If you do not have a plan, then you're planning to fail. With that being said, if you plan on being a successful cheater and keeping your good man status then you have to plan accordingly.

To plan accordingly, you have to know your woman and child/children schedule. You have to know when your family is going to be at home and when they plan to be out and about. You don't want to be out with your mistress and you see your woman and child/children, then you have to hide or change directions at a moment's notice so they won't catch you red handed.

Know where your woman is at all times. If your woman is at work, make sure you know what time she goes to lunch and where she is going for lunch if she leaves the office, especially if you both work different shifts. If you are off and your woman is at work, be smart if you plan on seeing your other woman.

When you wake up in the morning the first thing you should do is clean up as good and fast as possible. Prepare whatever you plan on cooking for dinner. This will make your woman believe that you have been home all day because the house is clean and dinner is made when she walks through the door.

Call your woman and ask her what time she is going to lunch and offer to bring that lunch to her. Or if she is hell bent on leaving the office, take her to lunch so when you take her back to work you know that she is secure back at the job which leaves you time to roam freely.

Let your mistress know what your plan is the day before. This will give her enough time to get herself together so that when you get to where she is, there will be no time wasted. Remember, she may be your mistress, but believe that she is still living her life when you're not around. Don't be fooled into thinking that she is sitting around waiting on your call, she may say that she is, but most likely she not. Don't just pop up and get disappointed.

When you get to your mistress don't waste a lot of time with small talk. Call her on the phone on the way over. Let her talk to you about all the small things that she needs to get off her chest, so when you get to her it can be all about business.

As you walk thought the door, make sure that she knows how much time that you have and that you will not be deviating from that time table before you even get into it. Once everything is clear and agreed upon, then you make sure you give it to her exactly the way she wants it with the time you have. Leave her wanting you more and anyone else less.

When it's time for you to wash up, do not, I repeat do not use any hygiene product that you do not have at your own home. If you use dove at home, use dove at your mistress house. But my suggestion on this matter is not to use any soap product at all. I know that you're thinking "what is the point in that?" or "that has to be the nastiest thing that you have ever heard". Well I'm going to put you up on game that was taught to me by an old Asian lady back when I was a youngster. Take a wash rag and turn the faucet on hot. Let the hot water run until it is so hot that the water starts to steam. Put the wash rag in the water and then immediately wipe your balls and then rinse the wash rag off and then wash your penis. The hot water will kill any odor causing bacteria. The temperature may be unbearable but it's a whole lot better than that conversation you're going to have if you go home smelling like fresh soap and water.

After you're done with your mistress make sure you make it back home before the child/children get out of school. If you need to pick the child/children up from school or the bus stop, make sure your there on time. You don't want the child/children to tell mommy that the teacher had to sit with them because daddy was late or the school call your woman asking what time the child/children going to be picked up.

Avoid all that confusion and questions by being on or before time. If you don't have to pick the children up start preparing dinner so when they walk through the door the child/children can see the great father that they have and can bear witness to mommy that daddy was home when they got there and was cooking dinner. If you know women like I know them, they are going to ask the child/children if daddy was home when they got there.

Make sure the child/children get started on their homework before they do anything else so when your woman comes home, everything will be handled and you look like the loving, good man that she loves to come home to. For the men that don't have child/children, just concentrate on getting home before your woman and making sure dinner is waiting on her. The main purpose for your actions is to make your woman believe that you have been home all day making sure she is happy when she returns home.

If your woman and/or child/children have extracurricular activities outside the house, make sure that you are always available for those activities unless you can't because of work, actual work. Don't use the excuse that you have to work so you can skip out on the activities so you can spend time with your mistress, it will back fire on you and how to handle this will be discussed in an upcoming chapter.

As a man, you want to be seen in the community as a man. There is nothing more attractive to a woman than a man who spends time with their child/children. Your woman will feel so lucky to have you and other women that don't get that same attention from their "baby daddy's" or men at home will fine your irresistible.

The more time that you spend with your family in and outside the home, the easier it will be on you when you're away from the home to relax and do what you do. Again, planning is a major component in most of the things that we do in life. The better you plan, the more success you will have as a good man and a successful cheater.

There is one more issue with planning I have to address. Men, I know that we use many excuses to leave the house to get what we want but there is one excuse that needs to be used one time and one time only. This excuse is the "I have to run to the store" excuse. Many men use this excuse to run and go get you a quickie or meet up with your mistress. If you use this excuse more than once and it happens about the same time every time you use it, be sure that your woman is going to get suspicious. You have to realize that the moment you step out that door your woman is timing you to see how long it's going to take for you to go to the "store" to get that last minute item you "forgot" to get earlier. Your woman knows how long it takes to go to the store. If you take longer than she thinks it takes to drive to the store, purchase that item and drive back home, you're going to have a problem even if it's not spoken of at that moment.

On another note, if you're going to use the excuse "I have to run to the store" and your plan blows up in your face by your woman and/or child/children wanting to go to the store with you, do not, I repeat do not change any of your mannerism. Do not tell them that they can't go to the store with you when any other time it would be perfectly fine. You must allow them to go so there won't be any question why you need to go to the store alone at this point in time. This is what you need to do, go to the bathroom, text your mistress code 33, which means that you are not going to be able to make due to circumstances not in your control. Your mistress must understand and know a thing like this is going to happen and she must be willing to accept this if she expects to be in your life. Plan ahead so you won't fall behind.

Chapter 3-Always be open and true

Being open and truthful when living the life as a cheater sounds like an oxymoron. But if you're going to be a successful cheater and still remain somewhat of a good man, you have to be honest with yourself, your woman and your mistress. I know you're probably thinking that I must be off my rocker to be honest and still get away with being a cheater. Well let me explain what I'm trying to say in detail about this topic of discussion.

First and foremost you have to be honest with yourself. Ask yourself if cheating is really going to fix the problem that you are having in your life. If you're attempting to cheat on your woman and you're a good man, there has to be a problem. If you're considering taking the risk of being a cheater and losing everything that you have built with the woman that you are with, then there is a problem.

So look at yourself, really break yourself down and see what the problem is and if this problem can be fixed through other means besides becoming a cheater then do so. But if you can't find a solution to the problem and you can't find a problem with yourself, then continue reading.

Be truthful and honest with your woman about all your wants and needs. One problem that men who decide to cheat have is that they are not totally honest with their woman about all the things that they want and need that turns them on and makes them happy. If your woman could totally fill each and every one of your mentally and physical desires, I don't think that a man would have a need to go out and get extra when he has plenty at home. Your woman is supposed to be your best friend and you "should" be able to tell her anything without being judged. Now if you can't do that, you may need to think about re-evaluating your relationship and she may not be the one for you.

Before you go outside the house, try talking to your woman. Let your woman know everything that you would like to try sexually with her. Like I said before, she is your best friend so don't be afraid of what you have on your mind. She should be understanding and considerate of how you're feeling. And if she's a good woman, she will appreciate you being honest with her and will love you much more. I'm not going to lie to you; this conversation will redefine your relationships for better or for worse.

If you're a man that has a certain fetish for nurses, ask your woman if she could dress up in the nurse's uniform you got from Sara's Secrets. Ask her if she could check your temperature through the thermometer in your pants. Let your woman know that if you like a little pain and you want her to spank you every once in a while for being a bad boy. And if you're into this, not many men are, but some are, but if you want your woman to place a toy into your back side area because you like the way it feels, let her know so she can decide if that is something that she would be willing to do for you.

Being honest with your woman will free up your mind and will also let you know where your relationship stands. If your woman is willing to do the things that you enjoy then you have a woman that loves you and is willing to do anything to keep you happy and your relationship together. If this is true, then there really isn't a reason for you to step out. Now if she doesn't agree with what you want and need, and you have more to lose by leaving the relationship than staying, then cheating may be the course of action that you may-need take for your total happiness and fulfillment.

Ok, you had the conversation with your woman and you decided that you are going to cheat and you found the woman that you are going to have this affair with. This is what you need to do to have success as a cheater. Be truthful with your mistress about your current situation, future intentions, and your wants and needs.

Being truthful with your mistress about your current situation is very important. Let your mistress know that you are in a relationship from the first conversation that you have with her. Don't lead her on and have her believing that you are single and may be the man for her and only her. This will eventually blow up in your face when she finds out that you have a woman. And believe me, if you're with this woman for more than a month time period, she will find out.

Let her know that you are in a relationship and that you love your woman, but you find her very attractive. Let her know that there is something about her that has you interested and even though you know you're wrong, you want to get to know her in a more personal way. Now with that being said, she will have to decide whether this is something she will consider or leave you alone completely. But at least you gave her the option to choose and then ball is in her court.

If she chooses to be your mistress, let her know what you need and want from her so she can further decide if she is willing to participate. Whatever you talked to your woman about and she decided that she couldn't or wouldn't do for you then it's your mistress's job to fill in. So explain to her what your woman is not willing to do and ask if she is willing to do whatever it is for you. Explain to her what you can do for her if she is willing to do one or multiple things for you. It's kind of like a verbal contract stating, this is what I'm willing to do for you if you do this for me. If either side doesn't uphold their side of the deal, the verbal contract is broken and both sides will part ways without any further obligations.

When you are honest with everyone you will be free of guilt. With your woman, you tried being open and honest with her. You fulfilled your obligation as her man to come to her before doing anything outside the house. So with that being said, no need to feel guilty about "doing you". Also, being honest and upfront with the woman you want to cheat with will free you from the guilt of lying and this will open your mind up to what

you need to concentrate on and that's becoming a
successful cheater and a good man.

Chapter 4-Don't do more for your mistress than you do for your woman

We discussed being open and honest with your woman. If you're still reading this book then you still are considering being a good man and a successful cheater. No matter your reason for cheating, you have to realize that in order to be a successful cheater you will always have to keep your woman first.

Ok, when I say "keep your woman first", I mean you have to do for your woman before you do anything for yourself. It is essential that she feels this way. If she doesn't feel like she is your one and only, you will always have to answer questions like "where are you going?" or "how long will you be gone?" As a man that wants to get his extra on the side, you can't be bothered with little emotional side tracks. Your woman should never have to question where she stands in your life.

When you're home with your woman you have to make her believe that your world revolves around her. She has to believe that she is the reason that you get up in the morning and the reason why you work so hard. When you're at the house, do everything that she wants and needs like we discussed in the earlier chapter. Make sure you do a lot of errands for the house without being asked. When you do this she will always suspect that you're doing the right things in and out the home.

When you're outside the home you have to work harder at letting your woman know that you are all about her. When you're at work send her a text stating that she is on your mind. Call and check in periodically. Ask your woman if she needs anything while you're out. These small gestures will have your woman feeling secure and will free you up to do what you want to do.

Do not ever get your situation twisted. Your woman is your woman and your mistress is your mistress. These roles are not interchangeable. Do not, and I repeat, do not do more for your mistress than you do for your woman.

The key rule is to do two times as much for your woman than you do for your mistress. If you're going to pay a bill at your mistress house, you better be paying the all or majority of the bills at home with your woman. If you're going to buy flowers for your mistress you should buy her a half of dozen and your woman should get a dozen. If you are buying your mistress a box of candy then your mistress gets the small box and your woman gets the big box.

This rule is essential to keeping the balance of who comes first in your head so you won't get some crazy idea that your mistress means more to you than your woman. If you ever get to this point in your relationship, go back to chapter three and have a talk with your woman about how you're feeling about your relationship and be honest about what you want and need from her to do for you. If you're not prepared to do that, then keep your emotions in tack or end your relationship with your mistress. If your woman isn't number one in your heart, then there is no reason for you to stay with her.

When you're cheating you have to remember the roles that you have established. You also have to remind the mistress of what her role is. Women love competition just as much or maybe more than men do, especially when it comes to proving how much more of a woman they are compared to another woman. Your mistress already has the inside track over your woman because if you followed the instructions of chapter three and let her know what your woman isn't doing, she is going to do those things as well as she can do them.

She is doing this not only to make you feel good, but she is doing this to prove how much better a woman she is compared to your woman. And she will verbally and physically remind you of this when she is doing for you what your woman is not doing. In a way you will set yourself up for failure if you don't emphasize what her role is in this relationship, also, when you are making this statement out loud you're reminding yourself where your true allegiance lies. This will get even harder to deal with the longer you have a relationship with your mistress.

You have to remind yourself that you're not around your mistress long enough to see what kind of woman she would be to you if she was your main lady. She will be so driven by taking you away from your woman that she will be willing to do anything, but what would happen if she finally has you? Will she change? Will she stay the same? These are some important questions that you won't really know the answers to until you make the move from your woman to her. That is a big gamble. You have to think about the other lives that will be affected by your decision.

You have to be smart about the decisions you make. For the most part, there is no turning back once you leave your relationship especially if you leave your woman for another woman. If you leave because you two just didn't make it and then once you are separated from her you found out that you couldn't live without her, a woman would respect that and may be willing to give the relationship another try. But if you leave your woman for another woman, and you and that woman don't work out and then you try to come back home, HELL KNAW! But if she does let you come back home after you left her for another woman, be very cautious. The way the relationship was before you left will never be the same. You might want to sleep with one eye open because this woman has been scorned, not by another man, but by you. Hell has no fury like a woman scorned. She may be allowing you to come back home so she can get you back for what you have done to her and if you have child/children, what you have done to them also.

Think about it, not only did you turn your back on your woman, you also turned your back on the child/children for something that was not guaranteed. Your woman should never be an option, your woman and family should always be your main choice. So when it comes to this situation, it is always best to get your own place and try to work the "I can't live without you" angle from a distance. But to avoid all this confusion and spending unnecessary money on moving, just remind your mistress and yourself what her role is, stay home with your family and remain a good man that successfully cheats.

Chapter 5-Make as little changes to yourself and home as possible

Whenever you add or change something in your life, it's pretty hard not to change the way that you conduct yourself. But if you want to become a successful cheater you have to know that people, especially your woman, are observing you at all times. If you recognize this or not, everyone in your life knows your likes, dislikes, what you do and what you don't do. So when you bring a mistress into your life, know you have to try your best not to change who you are and what you do.

I've seen this time and time again. When a person, man or woman, steps outside of their relationship, they tend to change the normal things that they do in their everyday lives. Men, we are notorious for doing this. If we find a woman that we want to impress, we completely try to reinvent ourselves. One day out of the blue you come home to your woman and you tell her that you want to start working out again, but you haven't worked out in fifteen to twenty years, she knows something is up.

Here's another one, you have never ever been into poetry, now all of a sudden you want to go to poetry readings on your way home from work by yourself, something is up. Women are suspicious by nature, now you go and give her a reason to investigate your actions, you don't want this at all. First and foremost, you should have a hobby or some things that you do outside the house to free yourself up for what you need to do. You should have this established from the beginning of your relationship, but we will discuss that in an upcoming chapter.

So, I guess the question is "what can I do not to in order to keep everything the same?" Well, recognizing that you need to watch your actions is a start. If you're a man that likes to watch a certain TV show or sporting event the same time of year, week, day, and hour, make sure you stay true to that. As soon as you miss that favorite thing you like to do at home, the same thing that you have been doing for years because you're doing something outside the house alone, there is going to be a problem starting to brew up under your feet. You will have to make time around all the things you do normally around the house so no one will question who, what, where, and why when you're away from the house. When you're cheating you want to draw as little attention to yourself as possible.

One of the major mistakes that a person makes when they decide to cheat is they lets their attitude change. When a man or woman conscious starts to eat at them because they know that they are doing something wrong, they tend to vent their frustration and confusion towards the people in their home. Their patience towards the spouse and/or child/children become so low that when you ask them a simple question like, "do you know where the butter is?" they explode like you asked them a question about quantum physics or what makes the Earth orbit around the Sun.

You have to be mindful of how you react to things and keep it the same. If you were always the patient parent or very patient with your woman, stay that way. If cheating is getting to you emotionally, maybe cheating isn't for you.

But if you think cheating is for you then you must keep your emotions under wraps. There are many ways to do that. One thing that we discussed in the prior chapter is keep reminding yourself of the purpose of why you're cheating. Make sure you keep your feelings in check when it comes to your mistress and keep your mistress in check by reminding her of what her role is in your life.

Don't overextend yourself by trying to balance your home and your mistress. The less outside stress you put on yourself, you're more likely to keep your emotions intact. When your emotions are under control then your mind can stay level and steady.

As you can see the majority of this chapter is referring back to the prior chapters on what you need to do not to change who you are and how you conduct yourself at home. You have to keep your routine steady. Whatever your routine is during the week, just don't change it, period. The home comes first. Your woman and/or child/children come before anything you do outside the home. Keep yourself in check and you will be successful at being a good man that cheats.

Chapter 6-Show and tell your woman how special she is at least three times a week

This chapter is very essential to your success at being a good man. Because before you can be a success at being a good cheater, you first have to be a success at being a good man. Many of us men go about our lives ass backwards. Since women pretty much outnumber men this day in age, it's not hard to have multiple of women in our lives. So we go around bouncing from woman to woman, getting what we want and need then split. After a while it starts to affect how we look at relationships as a society. Not only when we leave the woman, if we have children by this woman, then children are left also. When this happens, the hope of having a traditional family looks dimmer and dimmer as we go through each new generation.

This action leaves a negative effect on the woman and the children. The outlook on the traditional family has changed so much that it's hard to think of it as being traditional, but more of outdated and hard to achieve. So men, please, before you go out and do you, take up that old school mentality that the man must take care of the home before he takes care of himself.

Practice on being a good man and teaching your son to become a good man who takes care of home. Show your daughter the example of what a good man is supposed to be so when she is old enough to choose what kind of man she wants in her life, she has a better example. But it starts with your woman. Work on being a good example of what a man is supposes to be to your woman. Become successful at being a good man, before you attempt to be a success at cheating.

In order to be a good man to your woman, she has to be 100% secure in her role in your life. The way that you do this is by expressing how you feel about your woman in a series of ways. You have to tell your woman with your words how you feel. You have to spend quality time with your woman. You have to show how you feel about her though your actions. Also you have to show her how you feel through simple gifts. Do these things at least three times a week. When I say three times a week, I actually suggest more because you never really know what kind of attention she is getting at her job or in the streets when you're not around. You have to make sure your woman is all about you.

Expressing how you feel through words is more than saying a line of words that make her blush. This is a good start, but in order for you to succeed at expressing yourself to your woman and making her truly feel you, then you have to go deeper. When your woman is getting ready for work or you're on your way out the door to work make sure you tell her that you love her. I don't mean the "I love you" that you say to her that feels routine and dry, no like I said before; you have to do more to make it feel sincere rather if you feel that way or not. Remember, this ultimately comes back to what you need.

So when your leaving out the house or the bedroom on your way to work, walk out the door, then walk back in and say "baby, don't forget that I love you more than you know" then proceed to work. Call your woman on your lunch break and tell her "baby, I didn't want anything, just wanted to let you know that I was thinking about you". You should do these three times a week, but I suggest doing this three times a day. But not at the same time every day, make it random so she won't get used to it happening and get bored with it. Keep her guessing at all times in your relationship.

Another way you can express how your feel to your woman is spending time with her. In the morning, don't wake up with just enough time to shower, shit and shave then hit the door on your way to work. Wake up with enough time to have a conversation with your woman and/or child/children before you leave for work, your woman leave for work, and/or the child/children leave for school. If the type of job you have allows you to eat lunch with your woman, do that. And if you can't, call and ask your woman how her day is going while you're on your lunch break.

When you get home, if schedule allows it, you, your woman, and/or child/children should have dinner together. It doesn't have to be at the table, it can be in the living room watching TV. As long your spending time together that is all that counts. Help your woman with the dishes. Let her tell you about her day and what's on her mind. Later on that night, before you go to bed or get it on in the bedroom, have a little pillow talk with your woman. Give your woman that quality time that she needs so she know that you care for her.

Express how you feel about your woman through your actions. I have given you some examples on how to do this, but I'm going to give you a few more. If you're leaving before your woman or you wake up after your woman is already gone for work, write a note to your woman the night before. Tape it on the bathroom medicine cabinet mirror expressing how much you care about her and wish for her to have a good day. This will be the first thing that she sees in the morning and this little action will make her feel special because you took this time to do this for her. She might surprise you with a special treat of her own before leaving the house. Another way to express how you feel through action is if you can get to her job during your lunch break, put a card that expresses the way you feel about her on her driver side door so when she gets off work that will be waiting on her to brighten her day. Actions speak louder than words.

A simple gift can go a long way when it comes to expressing how you feel to your woman. Something as simple as ironing your woman's clothes for the next day or bringing her breakfast in bed will make your woman feel like the most important woman in the world. Bring your woman one single rose when she is feeling a little down. If it's that time of the month and you know she's feeling bloated and frustrated, rub her feet, buy her some pain pills, and break out the heating pad so she can relax. Let her know that you are here for her. She will appreciate the simple gifts like these as much or maybe more than diamond ear rings.

You have to be able to express how you feel to your woman at least three times a week so that she knows that you truly care about her. Your woman must always come first in your mind, body, and soul before you go out and do what you want to do. Peace in your house only comes from having a woman at peace. It's going to take a lot of hard work and time to accomplish this, but if you're going to be a success at being a cheater, you have to first be a success at being a good man.

Chapter 7-Have a hobby

To be a good man and a successful cheater you have to use checks and balances so you can be away from the house for long periods of time without drawing any suspicion to what you are doing and where you are at. The best way to make this happen is to have a hobby. Your hobby has to be something that you have done for years but not something that you do every day. You can't pop up one day and tell your woman that you have a new interest in pottery and don't think that she won't wonder where this new interest came from.

The reason why having a hobby is a must is because this will allow you to be excused from the house for an uninterrupted period of time. Your woman and/or family should know that on certain days of the week you're going to be gone doing your hobby and you will be back after you are done. You have to make sure that this hobby is well established before you start substituting it for your mistress. What do I mean by this? Say for instance, you like to go running at a park trail in the evening time. Your woman must witness you doing this hobby and enjoying it for her to relax and let you have your "me" time. Your hobby should not be done every day. Like I said before, this hobby should be established early in your relationship in order to make it stick.

Your hobby should be something that takes up a good amount of time so you will have plenty of time to set up your meeting with your mistress. If your hobby is at the gym, you should at least be there for two maybe two and a half hours. Think about it, forty-five to sixty minutes cardio, then lower or upper body depending on the day and throw in shower time, oh I forgot about drive time. All this must be calculated correctly in order for this to work for you.

So let me show you how to substitute it. You drive to the gym, get on the tread mill for about fifteen minutes to work up a good sweat. About this time your mistress should be there. Depending on what you have planned for the day either she can work out with you or you go back to her apartment or house to do what you do. Make sure you leave your car at the gym just in case your woman decides to drive by to see if you are actually there. Selection of a mistress with her own place is major. I will explain why this is so important in a chapter to come. Once you get to her place use the hot water and wash rag trick to clean up then you two can do your thing for about thirty to forty-five minutes. Hot wash rag again then have her drive you back to the gym. Go back in and do some free weights to get a nice pump then you hit the shower.

After you're done taking a shower, clothed, and ready to go, get in your car and call home to let your woman know that you're on your way. Ask her do she need you to pick up anything before you get there.

After you make that phone call home, call the mistress and let her know that you're heading to the house. On your way home it's good to "converse" with the mistress and let her know how much fun you had and you can't wait to do it again. Do not talk to her the whole way home. Before you get three miles away from home your conversation with her should be over.

Before you end the phone call remind her that you are almost home, so no more phone calls or texts unless you text her first. But as a good man you should not be contacting her from home unless it's an emergency. When your home, there is nothing else that exist, period. Make sure you have her number memorized because once that phone call is over; it should be deleted out of the phones memory. This too will be discussed in an upcoming chapter.

There are many examples of what you can do to substitute your hobby to be with your mistress. Now, remember, remember, and remember, your hobby should be something that does not interest your woman and/or child/children. If you have a child/children, make sure your hobby isn't age appropriate for child/children. That is the easiest way to eliminate child/children out of the deal. If you truly have read this book and follow the guidelines laid out for you, then you should really know your woman. With this in mind, you should know what your woman likes, dislikes, and interest. So if you know all this then it will be easy to know what hobby you can choose that she is not interested in.

If your woman doesn't like to be outside or get her hands dirty, you may want to choose working on cars as your hobby for an example. Working on cars or the restoration of cars is a great hobby to have. You can be gone at junk yards for hours looking for the part that your need. It's dirty and not many women want to hang around a junk yard on their day off, plus it can be too dangerous for children to go. So this is how you can substitute junking to see your mistress.

Before the weekend comes make sure your woman knows that you plan on working on your car and you plan on going to the junk yard. You do this to get conformation that there is nothing that your woman needs help with and it doesn't look suspicious like it would if you tell her last minute. After you get conformation from your woman, text code 36 to your mistress then delete the message. Like before, your mistress should know the codes.

The day you go to the junk yard make sure you go early so your woman won't change her mind and try to multi task with your time. What do I mean by this? Well she will ask you if she can come with you so she can do some shopping after you look for your part. If you get up early, the child/children are probably still asleep and she would rather wait until later than wake the child/children up early, plus the malls and most stores don't open until 9 am.

Make sure you put on your raggedy, stained clothes. When you leave the house, wait until you're a good three miles away from the house then call your mistress and let her know that you are on your way. When you get outside your mistress's place, call your woman and let her know that you have made it to the junk yard and your phone is going to be in your car. Leave your phone in the car and go have some fun with your mistress. Don't stay too long, remember, timing is everything.

When you leave your mistress's place check your phone to make sure your woman hasn't called. If she called check the message to see if it's an emergency. If not proceed to the junk yard. If you plan on looking for a car part for real then do so. But if you're only using it as a cover then go out to the yard and cover yourself with dirt, reach in a car engine and make sure your hands are dirty. Lay on the ground under a car so your back side can get dirty. After you are good and dirty, go to the car and call your woman. Let her know that you either found the part you needed or they didn't have the correct part that you needed and you are on your way home. Ask her if there is anything she needs. Call the mistress and let her know that you are on your way home. This should be a repeat of the prior call procedure.

When you walk through the door greet your woman with open, dirty arms and try to hug and kiss her. Most likely she will keep away from you and tell you to go take a shower. Take your shower and spend some quality time with your woman and/or child/children. If you do this correctly you can successfully cheat and remain a good man.

Chapter 8-Use good judgment on who you cheat with

There are many sources of where to find that special woman that you chose to cheat with. In this chapter we are going to talk about the women that you should steer wide from. This subject cannot be taken lightly if you want to be a successful cheater and still keep your good man status.

Every man in the world should know this first one, but as I can see there are some men out there that don't know the first rule of choosing the right woman to cheat with. Do not and I repeat do not try to cheat with any women that belong to your woman's family and none of her friends. I know what you are thinking, it's so easy to choose one of these women because you are around them all the time and you are already familiar with them so why not? For that particular reason is why you do not choose any family or friends. Too close to home. You want to keep your mistress and home as far apart as possible.

A woman will go behind a female family member for a man, it happens all the time. But as soon as you cross that woman, here comes the family. Always remember, blood is thicker than water.

Females can be really catty at times. If they see a female relative with something good, they get envious of that family member and on occasion will try to get what they have even if their intent is just to see how good this man really is. There are women in the world that have never had the privilege to experience what it feels like to deal with a good man that will treat them with respect. A woman will cross anyone to get a chance to see how it feels, even backstab her own family. So if you're going to remain a good man, reframe from falling into that trap. To your woman's family, she is your one and only true love and you will never disrespect her by cheating on her, especially with her own family. Keep the outlook as a good man and have your woman be the envy of the family.

"Friends, how many of us have them? Friends, ones we can depend on?" Whodini said it best. Females switch friends like dresses but this does not give you the right to help yourself to one of them. Motives my friend, please think about the motives. How would you feel if your friend tried to get with your woman? You would feel like they are not your friend and they were only after what you got. Switch that mentality around to your woman eyes and you will see that it's not for you. If you choose to do this, her friend has something to hold over your head and if you don't act right she can kill your whole world and she will not care. She would rather see her friend down and out than happy with you. Misery loves company, don't fall for the trap, I don't care how fine she is or how much she flirts with you. Matter of fact, if you really want to keep your good man status, when she first starts giving you the idea that she is into you, tell your woman. Yea I said it, snitch on her ass. Better to be a snitch in the beginning than a lying, cheating bastard when things get too far out of hand and her friend blows up your home.

Protect your neck and your home, stay away from her friends. If you really want to look like a good man, barely acknowledge her friends when they are around. If a group of her friends or her main friend is at your home when you get there, kiss your woman, say hi to the friend and retire to your bedroom until the friends are gone. To be a successful cheater you have to think above and beyond what's in front of your face.

No co-workers! I mean your co-workers and your woman's co-workers. A mistake in either of these areas can mess up your whole livelihood. You don't want to take a chance on losing your job or your woman's job because you couldn't keep your penis in your pants.

In any affair, they are eventually going to end and when they do end, it's not always pretty. So why make your workplace uncomfortable because you and the woman from accounting affair didn't work out. Both of you are not going anywhere and now you have to see her every day. Heaven forbid that your woman shows up on your job to see you. The looks that she will receive from this woman will draw questions into your woman's mind like "what reason does this woman have to look at me in this way?" This leads to doubt and you don't need that in your relationship. Not to mention if this lady starts to act unprofessional with you at your job. She may begin to argue with you or cause a scene in the workplace. You don't need to deal with that at work. The same thing goes for dating a woman at your woman's job. Your woman does not need any added stress on her job because of a bad decision you made. Work is stressful enough for your woman. The last thing she needs to worry about is a woman in the next cubical laughing and making sly comments about her. Your best bet is to stay away from co-workers. If things don't go right, it will be one hell of a Christmas party.

When it comes to your job, if you're going to be a successful cheater you need it more than all the knowledge coming out of this book. Finance keeps your woman happy and the mistress happy. If you don't have a job you won't be able to do for your woman and/or your mistress. If you don't keep the finances going then you're just another bum ass man in their lives that they don't need.

As easily accessible an ex's may be, do not choose an ex as your mistress. There is too much history there that may start to override your thinking after a while. Ex's are good for two things, to remind you of where you have been and remind you of where you're going. Yesterday is the past, today is a gift, that's why they call it the present. If you value yourself and what you and your woman are trying to build together, leave the ex's out of it. That's all I have to say about this point.

Now when choosing a mistress you have to know what

they are capable of when times get hard and you are not able to give them what they are asking for. This goes back to explaining the role that the mistress will have. If you have to remind her of what her role is because of her actions more than two times, then she may not be the mistress that you need. She has to be as intelligent as you when it comes to accepting and carrying out her role in your life. You don't need to have a woman that is jealous of your woman and what she has. As I explained in the prior chapter, yes you have to give to the mistress, but the mistress does not need to know what your woman is receiving. Keep those two lives very separate.

To keep the drama down, your mistress needs to know the bare minimum information about you. Really she doesn't need to know your last name. The last thing you need is a crazy woman looking up your information on the internet, then calling your home number or slowly driving pass your house so she can get a look at what the competition is receiving and she is not. K.I.S.S is the best course of action when choosing a mistress. Keep it simple stupid.

Using good judgment of who you cheat with is very important if you're going to keep the status of a good man. Stay away from family, friends, co-workers and exes. Also keep the information that you give out about yourself to a minimum. If you can do that then you are one step closer to being a successful man that cheats.

Chapter 9-Know your resources

The most common way to get caught cheating now a day is to be a man that does not know his resources and how to use them. I'm not talking about your homeboy that knows a girl that likes you; even though that is not a good way to find a mistress, leave friends and family out of your business. The resources that I am talking about are the ones we use on a daily basis to keep in contact with people in our lives. Computers, internet, and cell phones are some of the most common ways that we stay in contact these days.

If you're going to be a successful cheater and still remain a good man you have to be a thinking man. If you're going to use a computer, tablet, or net book to assist you in finding a woman that you would like to cheat with, you must know how these things work and how not to leave valuable information laying around for your woman to find. A computer, tablet, and net book are all called hardware. I can't explain computer hardware in depth right now, but I will let you know what you need to know not to get caught cheating when using these devices.

Whenever you use these devices they use memory that is stored in your device until it is deleted. Say for instant that you write a letter to your mistress using Microsoft Word program. After you are done writing the letter, you print it out and everything is fine. When you close the program, a message will come up asking if you want to save this file, click NO!

But if for some reason you saved the letter then you deleted it after you are done, good, but you're not done there. Whenever you delete something on your computer, it doesn't just disappear into thin air. All deleted items go to your recycle bin that is located on your desk top. Your desk top is the screen you see as soon as you log on to your device and the recycle bin is usually located in the far left top of the screen. If it is not located on your desk top, take you device to office depot, best buy or someone that has knowledge of computers so you can receive help locating it. It is essential that you know where this is.

Once you located the recycle bin, right click on it with your mouse or key pad and empty it. After it says that the recycle bin is empty, open it up and make sure that the file is gone before you walk away from your device. Doing this will save you a lot of head ache and explanations. Now there are other ways to recover files off your devices, but if your lady is knows all that, I don't think these devices should be used as one of your resources.

Using the internet is the most common way to get in contact with a new female now-a-days. This can be great tool if you know how to use it. The sites people are using to connect with each others are www.tagged.com, www.pof.com, and www.facebook.com.

Be very careful when using these websites unless you know every person that your woman deals with in her life and what they look like. You don't want to slip up and try to contact a female that knows your woman. My suggestion, if you feel like you need to use the internet to find a woman is to go to the adult sites that you have to pay to become a member. www.onlinebootycall.com and www.adultfriendfinder.com are two examples that you may want to look into. If you're going to pay for a membership, make sure you use a prepaid Visa or MasterCard. You don't want to use your known bank or credit card. Remember, you are not trying to leave a paper trail as evidence to what you are doing. Also, you should not be on these websites for more than a month. If you haven't found a woman on these sites by then, you may just want to stay home and save your money.

If a woman is paying to be on this site you know that she isn't playing about what she wants to do and she has some kind of income which will help you out in the long run. Most women on these sites will accept the fact that you have a woman and will be content on giving you what you need and want as long as you do right by them.

If you're going to use the internet, you have to get rid of any evidence that you have been on these sites. The way you do that is first off don't use any home devices to access these sites. And depending on your job's internet policy it may not be a good idea to access these sites at work.

A close friend or families house maybe an option. Don't

let them know what you're using their computer for, just ask if you can use it on your way home from work or while you're visiting them. Another option, get a library card and use the library internet. But if you have no choice but to use the internet at your house follow these instructions.

Whenever you use the internet, there is a favorites tab on the tool bar(if you don't know what that is, go to office depot, best buy or use www.google.com to find out) that saves all the sites accessed on what day and time. When you click on the tab it will open up to three subsections, favorites, feeds, and history, click on history.

When you do that it will give you three categories to choose from, last week, yesterday(whatever day that is), and today. Open each one and search for the websites that you have been accessing that you don't want anyone to know. When you find the website, put the mouse over it and right click. After you right click two selections will come up, expand or delete. Select delete. After you select delete it will ask you if you're sure that you want to delete this, select yes and now you're totally clear.

Cell phones, cell phones, cell phones, what can I say about cell phones? The invention of cell phones has helped man kind in more ways than I can mention. But cell phones is the number one way to get caught cheating if you don't know how to use it. With cell phone technology becoming more and more technical, you have to stay on top of knowing every little thing about this device.

If you're truly serious about cheating, I suggest getting a basic flip phone especially if you're not the technical type. But if you must have the most up to date smart phone to impress whoever, listen up. Mainly smart phones are basically mini computers that you can make calls. So go back to what I said it the first part of this chapter about deleting internet history, follow the same instructions, and restart your phone. Also go back to the prior chapter about scheduling your mistress around your hobby. The same rules apply. Memorize your mistress's number and delete all calls and text from your phone before you return home.

If your woman is really your woman, she knows more about you than you know. You may not have told her all the information that she knows about you on purpose or all at one time, but eventually everything comes out in time. Believe it or not your woman knows your social security number, birth date, address, year you graduated, what schools you have attended, where you bank at and possibly your account and/or card numbers. The reason I mention this to you is if your woman has a combination of three of these things, she can break any password that you have on this Earth.

Most of us men have caught on to our woman looking at our phone bill to see what numbers we have been calling, so the next logical thing to do is to stop the paper statements and get your bill sent to you in your email. This is very proactive, but like I said, if your woman has any of this information, she can get into your email and check your phone bill. So how do you get around this? Well you can use an email that she doesn't know that you have. When you access the email follow the prior instructions to delete this website from your history like before.

If you have a phone plan with your woman, well, using your phone to communicate with your mistress may not a good idea because she has full access to text messages and phone calls. Don't even try it.

If you look or act guilty, to your woman you are guilty. So men, please stop carrying your phone with you everywhere you go like you have something to hide. I can understand taking your phone to the bathroom while you're doing number two, but if you're going to the bathroom just to pee, taking a shower, or going in the kitchen to get a beer, you are wrong. Your woman will notice the moment you start walking around with your phone glued to your hand. She will also notice that you will not answer certain numbers when she is around you.

Locking your phone is another key that you are doing wrong. If your mistress knows the rules and you have read all the procedures leading up to this point, there will be no need for you to lock or carry around your phone. Your mistress should not call or text you while you are at home anyway. I don't care if the world is on fire and she is all alone. You can't do anything for her because you are with your woman and/or family and that comes first.

You should be able to leave your phone sitting anywhere

and dare your woman to look through it because you have nothing to hide. If you can't do that, you may not want to risk losing what you have by cheating.

Chapter 10-Last and most important things to know

I have given you a lot of do's and don'ts throughout this book. But to be totally honest with you, being a good man is hard enough job, why would you even want to add something as difficult like cheating into your life. The ultimate goal of being a good man is to build up your home and the people inside of it.

A good man is there for his son to make his son into a better man than he is. A man wants to pass on knowledge, rules, and guidelines to his son so that when he becomes a man and if he has a son of his own, he can teach his son the things that you have taught him. I mean positive things that will make his walk through life a little easier. A good man teaches his son to respect women the same way his father respected his mother. A good man teaches his son to cherish a good woman and know which type of woman is not good for him. A good man is the first and most important role model his son will ever have.

A good man is the first example of what kind of man his daughter will want to have in her life. A good man shows his daughter through his actions toward her mother of how a man should treat, love, and protect a woman. A good man should have conversations with his daughter and let her know how smart, beautiful, and important she is so she won't fall victim to the flattery from the first guy that tell her these things. A good man's daughter reply to that attention will be "I know that already because my daddy told me". When a good man does these things it will help his daughter have a better choice of what type of man she allows to come into her life.

A good man is there for his woman to make her feel like the most important, intelligent, beautiful woman on this Earth. A good man encourages his woman to be proud of whom she is and help her achieve more. A good man lifts his woman up when she's down and won't let anyone cause her any harm mentally or physically. A good man is his woman's support group, cheering section, and the best friend. A good man's woman should never have to go to anyone other than her man for what she wants and needs.

Why am I saying this? I'm trying to remind you of what your role is as a good man. There is so much that you are risking when you decide to step outside of your relationship and your home. The risks outweigh the reward when you start a life of a cheating man. If you look at the title of this book the first thing you read is A Good Man. Being a good man to your woman and/or family comes before you can succeed at anything else.

The first chapter talks about taking care of home. I think that it is important that we concentrate on that more than anything else in this book. So many men are absent from the home, this means the home isn't taken care of.

Instead of fixing what's wrong with our homes, we rather leave the home and try it again somewhere else when the problems at home are not that serious. Cheating rarely fixes anything. Cheating causes more problems in the long run.

But if you still want to cheat, even after everything that I have just said, let me tell you what to do if and when you get caught cheating. Tell the truth. I know you're thinking "why should I tell the truth?" You tell the truth because you got caught and no matter what you do or say, your woman is always going to have the thought of you stepping outside the home in her head. And when you lie, you have to tell another lie to keep the lie going, then tell more lies to cover that lie, after a while you're going to lose track of the lies and you're going to be right back where you started when you first got caught.

Tell your woman the truth, be honest, and let her know why you did what you did. If she loves you and wants to keep you in her life she will be willing to work through the problems that caused this infidelity. Counseling is a great way to approach all the problems going on within yourself and/or the family so you can correct the problem. Unless you talk about it and come up with a game plan to tackle the problem, it will never go away.

If you don't get anything else out of this book, take this with you. Through many "successful" and "unsuccessful" trials I have discovered what needs to be done to become a successful cheater and remain a good man. To tell you the truth, its takes too much time, money, and energy to do all these things in this book to remain a good man, and on top of that, not getting caught cheating. It's not worth it in the end fellas. If you have a good and true woman at home, get there and stay there.

Work with your woman to make your family life the way that you want it. Make your relationship to where everyone is happy and taken care of. We have too many children growing up without fathers to lead them in a positive way. We have too many women struggling to make a home on their own and choosing the wrong man to help them when the right man was there at the beginning. Let's leave the shacking alone and let's get back to building homes. If nobody else can testify to that, I can.